LET'S-READ-AND-FIND-OUT SCIENCE®

STAGE 1

Is All Around You

by Franklyn M. Branley • illustrated by John O'Brien

HarperCollinsPublishers

The *Let's-Read-and-Find-Out Science* book series was originated by Dr. Franklyn M. Branley, Astronomer Emeritus and former Chairman of the American Museum–Hayden Planetarium, and was formerly co-edited by him and Dr. Roma Gans, Professor Emeritus of Childhood Education, Teachers College, Columbia University. Text and illustrations for each of the books in the series are checked for accuracy by an expert in the relevant field. For more information about Let's-Read-and-Find-Out Science books, write to HarperCollins Children's Books, 1350 Avenue of the Americas, New York, NY 10019, or visit our website at www.letsreadandfindout.com.

Library of Congress Cataloging-in-Publication Data
Branley, Franklyn Mansfield, 1915–2002.
   Air is all around you / by Franklyn M. Branley ; illustrated by John O'Brien.–Newly illustrated ed.
      p.   cm. – (Let's-read-and-find-out science. Stage 1)
   ISBN-10: 0-06-059413-6 – ISBN-10: 0-06-059415-2 (pbk.)
   ISBN-13: 978-0-06-059413-8 – ISBN-13: 978-0-06-059415-2 (pbk.)
   [1. Air–Juvenile literature.]   I. O'Brien, John, date.   II. Title.   III. Series.
QC161.2.B7 2006   2004005043
551.5–dc22   CIP
                                                                                      AC

Typography by Elynn Cohen   1   2   3   4   5   6   7   8   9   10   ❖   Newly Illustrated Edition

That's hard to believe because you can't see the air or smell it. You can't feel it either, except when it's moving. Or when you spin around.

You can't see the air in a glass, but you can prove it is there. Try this experiment.

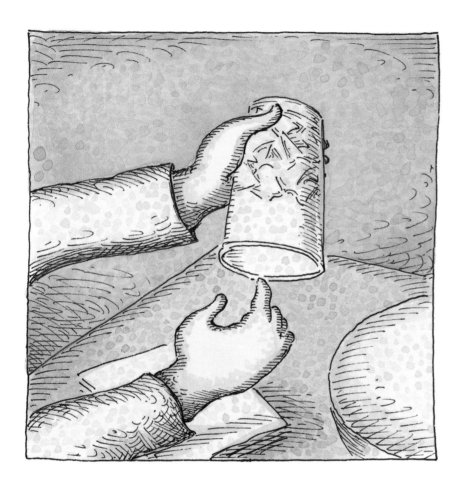

Stuff a paper napkin into the bottom of a glass. Turn the glass upside down. If the napkin falls out, stuff it in tighter.

Run a lot of water into the sink. Or put water in a big bowl. Color the water with a little food coloring. Not much, just enough to color it a little bit.

Keep the glass upside down. Make sure it is straight up and down. Do not tip it. Push it all the way under the water. Or as far under as you can.

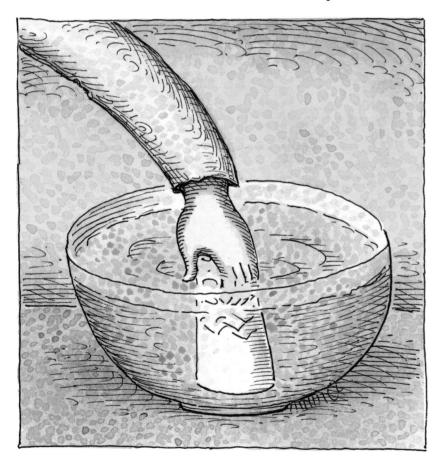

Lift the glass out of the water. Turn it right side up and take out the paper napkin. It is dry. The water did not touch it. The paper was under the water. But it did not get wet. Let's see why.

Once again put the napkin in the glass. Turn the glass upside down, and push it under the water.

Look at the glass through the water. The water does not go into it.

It can't go in because there is air in the glass. But you can make the water go in.

Tip the glass a little bit. A bubble of air goes out and up.

When the air goes out, there is empty space in the glass. Water goes in.

You can see it. The coloring you added to the water helps you see it. Bubbles go out, and water goes in.

Keep tipping the glass until all the air goes out. Now it is full of water and the napkin is soaking wet.

When the glass was full of air, there was no room for water.
When the air went out, the water went in.

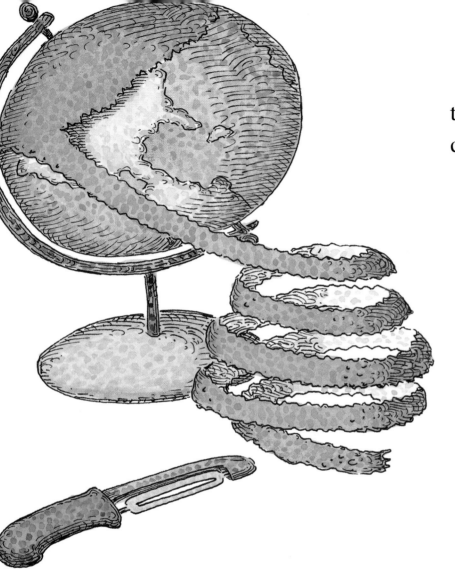

Air is all around you, and it is all around the earth. It covers the earth like peel covers an orange.

The air weighs a lot—5 quadrillion tons. That's 5,000,000,000,000,000 tons. That's hard to believe, but it's true.

The air in the room where you are weighs more than you think. In an average room, the air weighs seventy-five pounds or so. If the room is big, the air in it weighs more. If it is small, the air weighs less. We don't feel it because the air is spread all around us.

Airplanes and balloons fly in the air. But spaceships don't. Rockets push them higher than the air. Spaceships fly above the air that is all around the earth.

Spaceships must take air with them. They have enough to keep the astronauts alive.

When they go out of the ship, astronauts carry tanks of air on their backs. They need air to stay alive. And so do you and I.

Lucky for us, air is everywhere. Wherever we go on earth, there is air. Air is even in water. That's lucky for fish. The air is dissolved in the water. You can't see the air. But you can prove that it is there.

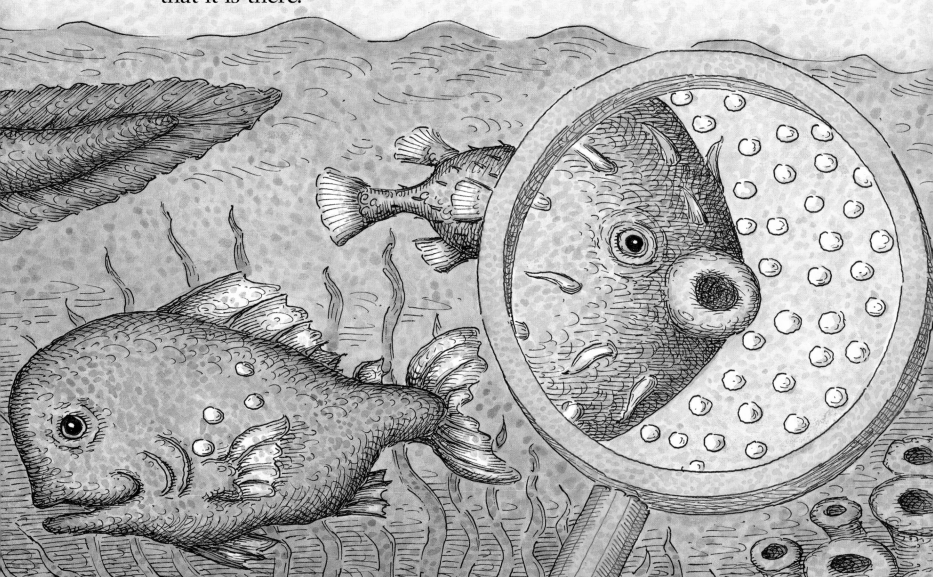

Fill a glass with water. Set the glass
aside and leave it for an hour.

After an hour you will see tiny bubbles on the inside of the glass. They are tiny bubbles of air. The air came out of the water.

Fish use the air that is dissolved in water. They have gills that help them do this. Air keeps them alive.

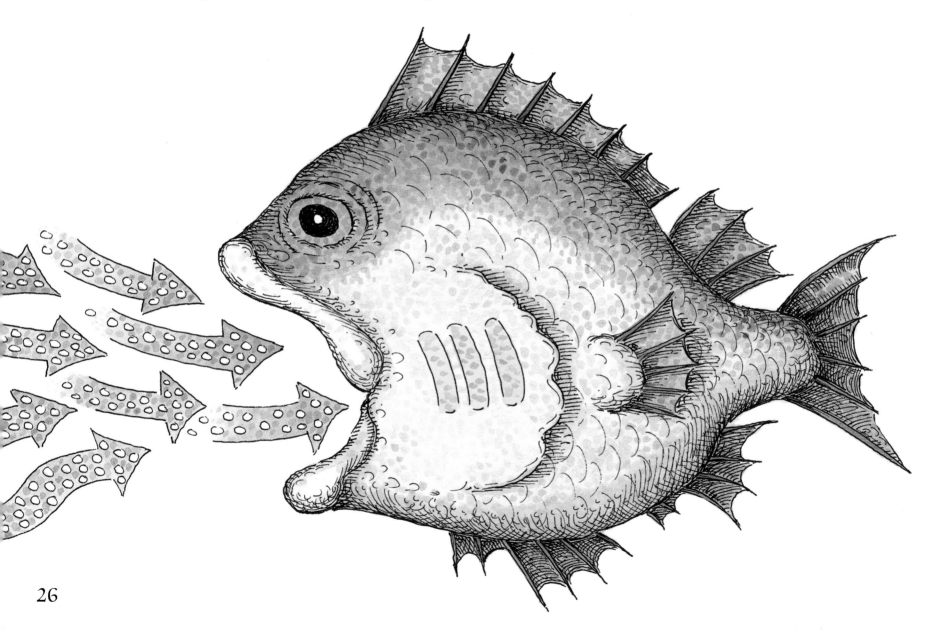

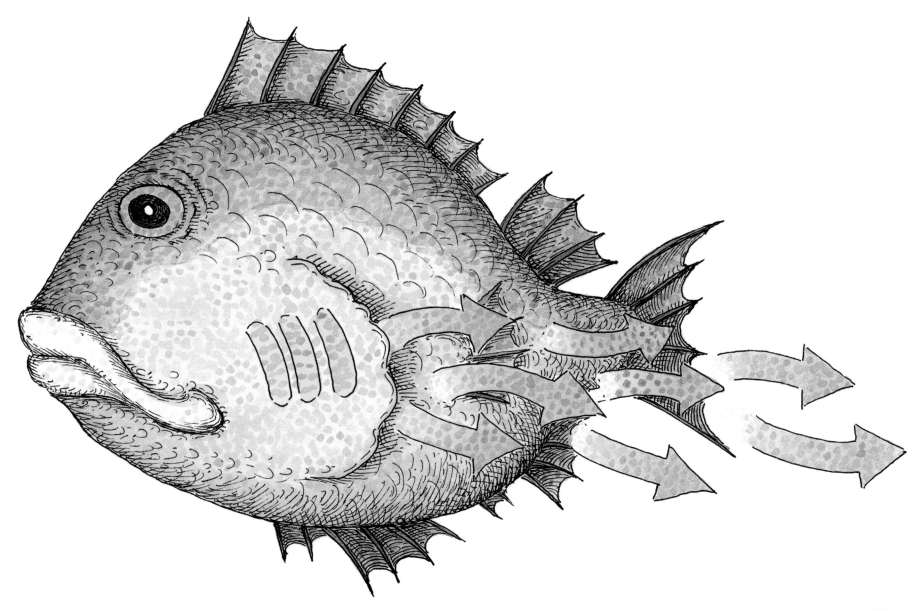

We can't breathe air that is dissolved in water. So when we stay underwater a long time, we have to take air with us. Divers take air in tanks strapped to their backs.

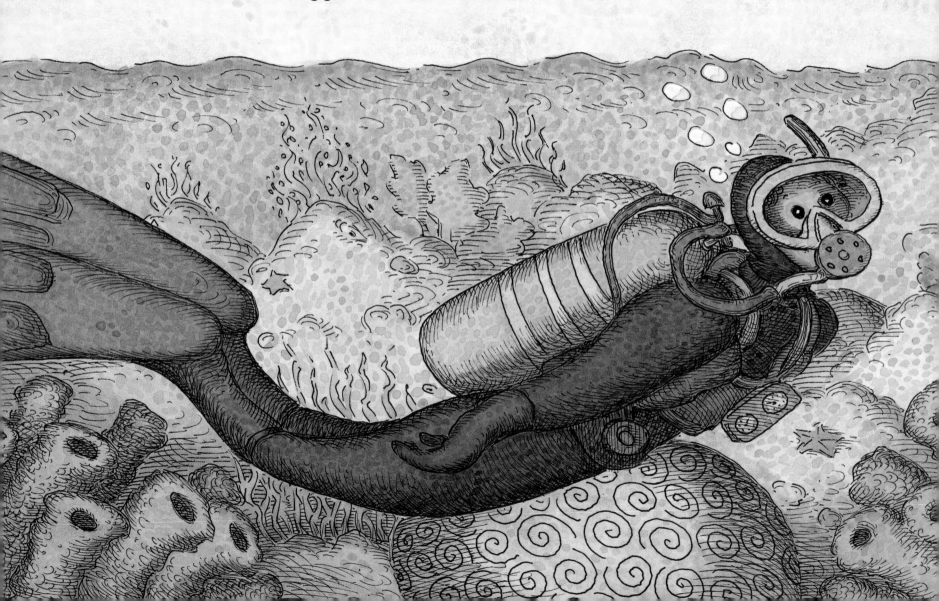

Air keeps us alive.

Wherever we go on earth—north, south, east or west, high on a mountain or deep in a valley—there is air.

Air is all around us.

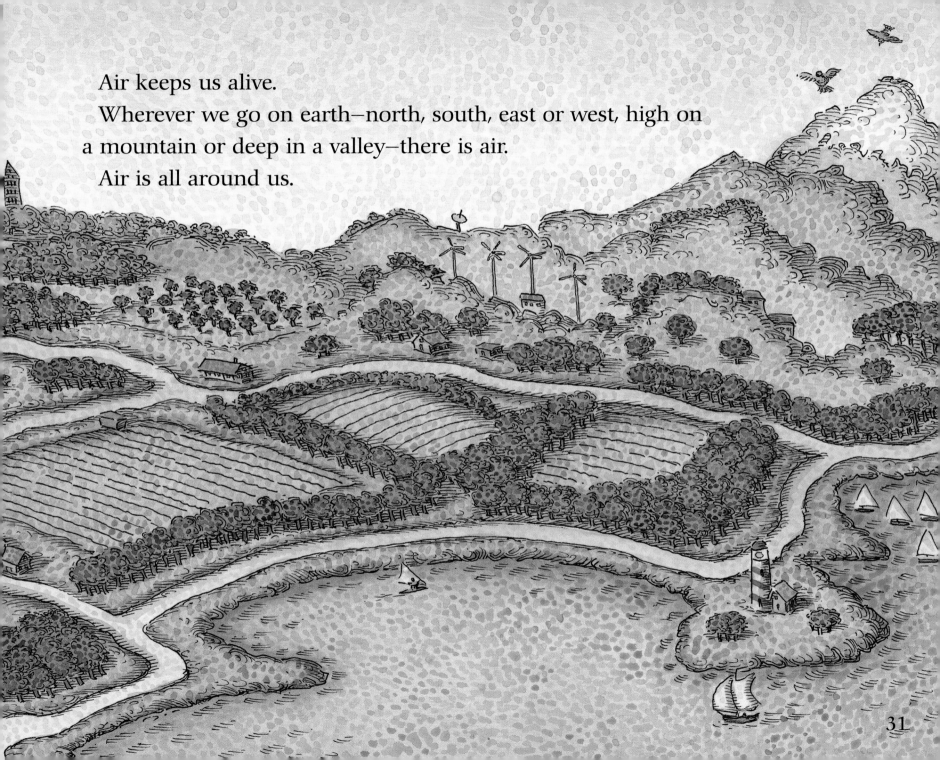

FIND OUT MORE ABOUT AIR

Air is all around, but we can tell it is there only when it is moving. Here are some ways to feel and see the air move.

- Spin around in a circle with your arms spread straight out and your hands open wide. Can you feel the air pushing past your hands?
- Next time you go outside, look at the clouds in the sky. Can you see them move? Air is pushing against them. What other things can you see air move?
- Pour some water into a clear glass. Then put a straw into your glass and gently blow air through it. You will see bubbles. They are made by air moving through the water.
- Turn on your family's hair dryer and hold your hand a few inches away. Do you feel the air as it is pushed out? Take a small slip of paper and hold it a few inches in front of the hair dryer. Can you see how the air pushes the slip of paper? Let the paper go and see what happens.

Air weighs more than you think. The air in a big space weighs more than the air in a small space. You can prove this with a balloon.

- Drop an empty balloon. It is heavier than the air and will fall straight to the floor. Blow air into the balloon. See the sides of the balloon stretch? Now you know it is full of air. Tie the open end of the balloon and toss it up over your head. This time the balloon will float gently down to the floor. The air inside the small balloon is lighter than the air in the big room.

All living things need air to live. Your body uses air in many ways. You breathe air in and out with your lungs.

- Breathe in. What happens when you pull air into your lungs?
- Breathe out. What happens when you push air out of your lungs?
- Hold your breath and count to five. How does it feel to fill your lungs with new air after you have been holding your breath?

There are many ways you can prove that air is all around. Can you think of some more?